My Mentoring Diary

My Mentoring Diary

Ann Ritchie
Paul Genoni

The Scarecrow Press, Inc.
Lanham, Maryland, and Oxford
in cooperation with
DocMatrix Pty Ltd, Canberra, Australia
2003

SCARECROW PRESS, INC.

Published in the United States of America
by Scarecrow Press, Inc.
A wholly owned subsidiary of
The Rowman & Littlefield Publishing Group, Inc.
4501 Forbes Boulevard, Suite 200, Lanham, MD 20706
www.scarecrowpress.com

PO Box 317
Oxford
OX2 9RU, UK

Copyright © 2003 by DocMatrix Pty Ltd
This 1st North American edition is based on *My Mentoring Diary: A Resource for the Library and Information Professions* / Ann Ritchie and Paul Genoni
DocMatrix Pty Ltd/2000.

All rights reserved. No part of this publication may be reproduced, stored in a retrieval system, or transmitted in any form or by any means, electronic, mechanical, photocopying, recording, or otherwise, without the prior permission of the publisher.

Library of Congress Cataloging-in-Publication Data
Ritchie, Ann.
  My mentoring diary / Ann Ritchie, Paul Genoni.
    p. cm.
  "This 1st North American edition is based on My Mentoring Diary: A Resource for the Library and Information Professions / Ann Ritchie and Paul Genoni DocMatrix Pty Ltd/2000."
  Includes bibliographical references.
  ISBN 0-8108-4684-5 (pbk. : alk. paper)
    1. Mentoring. I. Genoni, Paul. II. Ritchie, Ann. My mentoring diary (Canberra, Australia) III. Title.
BF637.C6R536 2003
158'.3—dc21   2002044668

∞™ The paper used in this publication meets the minimum requirements of American National Standard for Information Sciences—Permanence of Paper for Printed Library Materials, ANSI/NISO Z39.48-1992.
Manufactured in the United States of America.

CONTENTS

Using This Diary		3
My Mentoring Contacts		4
Section 1:	**Introduction to Mentoring**	
	What Is Mentoring?	7
	Why Is Mentoring Important?	8
	The Seven Stages of Mentoring	9
	NICE Analysis for Mentorees	11
	Setting Personal Objectives	13
	Making an Action Plan	14
	Making a Contract	18
Section 2:	**Learning Journal**	
	Introduction	23
	What Is Reflective Practice?	23
	What Is a Learning Journal?	24
	Learning Journal	25
Section 3:	**More about Mentoring**	
	Frequently Asked Questions (FAQs)	75
	Mentoring and Change	77
	Further Reading	79
	Organizations	80
Notes		81
About the Authors		83

USING THIS DIARY

My Mentoring Diary is a resource for mentors and mentorees in mentoring relationships, whether these are
- individual, peer, or group mentoring programs
- based in the workplace, in organizations, or provided by professional associations.

Its main purpose is to facilitate and record the learning which occurs in a mentoring relationship. The diary functions as
- a guide for conducting mentoring relationships—from the initial considerations of what the mentor or mentoree hopes to achieve by mentoring to the decision to conclude the relationship
- a journal to facilitate learning
- a record of mentoring activities as evidence for mentors' and mentorees' portfolios of continuing professional development.

Two key points underpin our philosophy of mentoring:

> The success of mentoring programs depends on all parties—mentors, mentorees, and the organizations and committees which support the program—sharing responsibility for making the program work.
>
> Mentoring is a two-way learning relationship, with benefits for mentors as well as mentorees. It is therefore important for mentors to see the experience as contributing to their own professional development.

MY MENTORING CONTACTS

My mentoring partner:
Phone:			(home)			(work)			(other)
Fax:			Email:

My mentoring committee liaison person:
Phone:			(home)			(work)			(other)
Fax:			Email:

Other contacts
Name:
Phone:			(home)			(work)			(other)
Fax:			Email:

Name:
Phone:			(home)			(work)			(other)
Fax:			Email:

Name:
Phone:			(home)			(work)			(other)
Fax:			Email:

Name:
Phone:			(home)			(work)			(other)
Fax:			Email:

SECTION 1

INTRODUCTION TO MENTORING

What Is Mentoring?

Mentoring is a form of professional and personal development which recognizes that we all learn from the experience, skills, and wisdom of others. In the classical form, a designated or self-appointed mentor assumes responsibility for the development of a learner, who is variously described as the mentoree (or sometimes mentee) or protégé. We prefer *mentoree* to *protégé*, as the latter implies the dependent, subordinate relationship of more traditional mentoring, and we believe that mentoring relationships are mutually beneficial and draw on complementary skills.

Kram and Isabella[1] describe the functions and roles of mentoring in these terms:
> Mentors provide . . . career-enhancing functions, such as sponsorship, coaching, facilitating exposure and visibility and offering challenging work or protection, all of which help the protégé to establish a role in the organization, learn the ropes, and prepare for advancement. In the psychosocial sphere, the mentor offers role modeling, counseling, confirmation, and friendship, which help the protégé develop a sense of professional identity and competence.

In recent years mentoring has evolved to include different types of relationships, for example:
- small groups of peers (called "co-mentoring" groups) with a learning-leader/facilitator, who come together for a particular learning experience
- the use of multiple mentors by one individual.

Whatever the exact relationship between the participants, three essential characteristics should be present in order to distinguish mentoring from other related forms of continuing professional development (e.g., coaching, training, preceptorship, internship). These are:

Mentoring is a two-way learning relationship which draws upon the knowledge and wisdom of experienced practitioners.

Mentoring fulfills two broad purposes—career and psychosocial development—with specific goals determined by the individuals involved.

Mentoring relationships develop over time and pass through several developmental stages.

These essential characteristics indicate that mentoring is a form of "deep learning." It is a highly personalized form of development, ideal for identifying and responding to learning needs which will not be met by generic training courses.

Why Is Mentoring Important?

Mentoring is a natural process, so organizations have three choices with regard to their level of support—they can ignore it, encourage it, or they can facilitate it by setting up and resourcing formal, structured mentoring programs. Mentoring can help develop the learning culture of an organization.

Generally, formal mentoring programs are created to orient or socialize people into an organization or a profession, or for ongoing training and development, both personal and professional.

Early in their careers, professionals ask how to pursue their continuing education. Professional associations increasingly try to measure continuing professional development (CPD) as a requirement for attaining and retaining enhanced membership status. One issue is how to identify specific programs and types of professional development which satisfy their criteria for continuing education. The issue for individuals is to select forms of training and development which not only satisfy their organization's requirements, but also meet their own personal needs.

Professional associations have long played a role in facilitating, endorsing, and certifying CPD programs. These take many forms—conferences, short courses, seminars, training programs, publication of professional journals and other literature, and study grants. These are valuable but they are, by necessity, broadly targeted at all members of the group, and their potential to meet the immediate needs of individual members is constrained.

Mentoring can overcome this limitation. Mentoring programs are immediately responsive to individual learning needs, and their availability to "members only" can be designated as one advantage of association membership.

Mentoring relationships typically create a "safe" learning environment. Practices which support individuals are consciously reinforced by mentors. These include targeting individual learning needs, addressing both career and psychosocial development needs, guaranteeing confidentiality, and facilitating recognition of individuals' successes and achievements.

The Seven Stages of Mentoring[2]

1. **Creation of rapport**

   Whether or not mentors and mentorees have already met, it is important that they spend some time at the beginning of the relationship getting to know each other. The aim is to develop a foundation of trust and personal respect, so be prepared to give enough time to allow this process to occur. Choose meeting places where you can talk and be relaxed. The official orientation to the program and training in mentoring skills will also facilitate the process.

2. **Formulate the main purpose and possible objectives**

   Organizations establish mentoring programs for a particular purpose—for example, to facilitate the professional socialization of new graduates or to orient new employees into a workplace. It is important to clarify your own reasons for wanting to be part of a program to ensure that they are compatible with the organization's objectives.

   Mentors and mentorees may discuss their goals in general terms at their first meeting. These topics may guide the discussion:
   - what you hope to achieve in your relationship (the main purpose)
   - ideas about activities to achieve this purpose (strategies or process)
   - when, where, and how often you will meet (in person, by phone, or by email).

   It is too early to decide about objectives, as you won't have had time to assess the situation, but you can probably make some agreements on the process and the types of activities you would like to do.

   At this stage you will probably find out enough about the other person or group members to decide whether or not you want to continue.

3. **Assess the mentoree's current situation**

   This defines the parameters of the relationship, which should be set by both the mentor and the mentoree, with the mentoree providing a self-assessment of their current situation. It is useful if the mentoree has thought about what they hope to achieve in the program. The NICE analysis on the following pages can be used to guide this discussion.

4. **Decide where you want to get to**

   The mentor helps the mentoree to set objectives and decide on an outcome and timeframe. A checklist is provided in *Setting Personal Objectives* on page 13.

5. **Choose a way of getting there**
   Discuss the objectives and options for achieving them, and turn these into an action plan by specifying tasks or activities for each objective. This is where the mentor's knowledge of the professional issues and experience in an organization or network are invaluable. Some factors are:
   - what are the mentoree's developmental needs?
   - what is the mentoree's preferred learning style?
   - what support is needed and available?
   - how and when can this support be accessed?
   - what are the obstacles?
   - what is the mentoree's level of confidence that the plan will be implemented, and how can this be increased?

6. **Do it**
   The mentoree implements the action plan, with help from the mentor at the regular meetings or when requested—for example, helping to focus on and observe relevant factors, giving coaching and feedback. (See also *Section 3: More about Mentoring*)

7. **Assess progress**
   The mentor helps the mentoree to overcome obstacles and to decide whether goals need fine-tuning or the method of achieving them needs adapting.

This process is cyclical, and steps 3 to 7 will be repeated. Where mentoring is part of an organization's formal program, mentors and mentorees may decide either to finish their relationship when the program concludes or to renegotiate the terms for another period.

Unlike other training methods, mentoring is generally understood to be a long-term, developmental relationship. Research shows that the benefits to mentorees are maximized in the two to five years after the initial phase and may also continue after the mentoring relationship has finished.

Since significant advantages accrue as a mentoring relationship develops, it is worthwhile continuing until there is agreement that it has reached a natural conclusion. Mentorees may then be ready to become mentors themselves.

NICE Analysis for Mentorees[3]

The NICE (Needs, Interests, Concerns, Expectations) analysis will help mentorees assess your current situations.

For mentors, the mentorees' responses to the questions in the NICE analysis can be used
- in your initial discussions, when you are working out the terms of your relationship
- as a guide to ensure that your own objectives are aligned with your mentorees' needs and expectations
- to stimulate ideas about opportunities for learning which will interest your mentorees. (See *Making an Action Plan*)

Needs

What do you need from a mentor and a mentoring relationship?

Interests

What are your main areas of professional interest?

Concerns

What are the main issues that concern you?

Expectations

What do you expect from your job or career?

And what do you expect a mentor to do for you in this respect?

Setting Personal Objectives

Your objectives can be as far-reaching and visionary as you like, but it is important that they are achievable within a certain time.

> An objective is a dream with a deadline

Having done a NICE analysis, mentors and mentorees are better able to discuss what they hope to achieve. Both the mentor and mentoree should set personal objectives—this acknowledges that mentoring is a two-way learning relationship and will help to focus strategies when the action plan is being formulated.

Use this checklist to guide you in setting objectives as the basis of an action plan. The acronym SMARTIS[4] will help you to remember these characteristics. Objectives should be:
  Specific
  Measurable
  Achievable and **A**ction-oriented
  Realistic
  Time-framed
  I-Statements
  Stretch

An Example

Here is my objective:

> *I will learn to be an excellent facilitator by the end of this year as measured by participant evaluation sheets.*

I will undertake the following activities to help me to achieve this objective:
- *I will set aside a weekly time to read the latest literature on training and facilitation*
- *I will ask my mentor to coach me in facilitation skills*
- *I will keep a learning journal*
- *I will start a toolkit of activities to draw on in facilitation sessions*
- *I will practice some form of physical exercise daily to maintain my fitness so that I can perform well in facilitation sessions*
- *I will enroll in a group facilitation course.*

Making an Action Plan

We suggest that mentors and mentorees both set personal objectives and then devote a meeting to discuss the activities which will help mentorees to achieve these objectives. Not all activities need to involve the mentors directly, as the mentorees must take responsibility for their own learning.

For mentors, the activities which will help to achieve your own objectives are most likely to involve developing a particular role which facilitates your mentorees' progress (e.g., coaching in specific skills, providing challenging opportunities, being a role model).

As well as developing your mentoring skills, mentors may also be interested in learning more about mentoring and how to facilitate mentoring programs.

The objectives I hope to achieve in my mentoring relationship are:

Objective 1.

I will undertake the following activities to help me to achieve this objective:

Objective 2.

I will undertake the following activities to help me to achieve this objective:

Objective 3.

I will undertake the following activities to help me to achieve this objective:

Objective 4.

I will undertake the following activities to help me to achieve this objective:

Objective 5.

I will undertake the following activities to help me to achieve this objective:

Making a Contract

After you have finalized your objectives for the mentoring relationship, you may wish to make a contract. Although not binding, a contract agreed on at the commencement of a partnership may be useful for several reasons:
- to communicate the mentoree's objectives to the mentor
- to remind the mentoring partners about their undertakings
- to make the expectations of both parties explicit
- as a statement of commitment and an indication that both partners take their responsibilities seriously
- to specify a starting date and expected finishing date to the partnership
- to remind both partners about the importance of reviewing their objectives and the nature of the partnership when the contract lapses.

If you wish to complete a contract, we suggest the following:

Date of Commencement:

Name of Mentor: Signed:

Name of Mentoree: Signed:

We agree to the following:

1.   Contact and meetings: *(Here outline the frequency and nature of the contact that is expected, and any restrictions regarding contact—e.g., neither party to be contacted during working hours.)*

2. Objectives: *(Here provide a summary of the mentoree's key objectives to be achieved through the partnership.)*

3. As the mentor I undertake to . . . *(Here summarize the responsibilities agreed to by the mentor in order to achieve the objectives—e.g., Introduce the mentoree to relevant networks and colleagues; Provide feedback on mentoree's progress on learning objectives; Advise on relevant professional reading.)*

4. As the mentoree I undertake to . . . *(Here summarize the responsibilities agreed to by the mentoree in order to achieve these objectives—e.g., Keep a learning journal; Seek out additional avenues of learning and skill development; Attend a relevant association meeting monthly.)*

5. Other: *(Here you may wish to include any other agreements of importance to the partnership—e.g., confidentiality.)*

6. Review of the mentoring partnership:
   We agree that this contract will be reviewed periodically, and at the latest no longer than 12 months after the Date of Commencement.

SECTION 2

LEARNING JOURNAL

Introduction

This section of *My Mentoring Diary* is a learning journal. Use these pages to
- record your meetings and activities
- write down your reflections and thoughts about your meetings
- relate your learning experiences to your objectives, action plans, and agreements which you have recorded in Section 1 of the diary.

Four pages per month have been provided—lined pages for notes and unlined pages for diagrams, pictures, or similar "creative" methods of recording or responding to your learning experiences.

My Mentoring Diary has been designed to encourage you to reflect on and learn from your mentoring. In general terms this is known as reflective practice.

What Is Reflective Practice?

Professionals often have to perform tasks for which they have not been specifically prepared by their education. It is part of their professional responsibility to react to these situations by making appropriate judgements which reflect their general expertise, knowledge, and skill.

One way in which a professional responds in these situations is to engage in what Donald Schön[5] calls "reflective practice." This is an activity in which the practitioner reflects, both in-action (during the event) and on-action (after the event), in order to improve his or her practice.

This means that professionals must be prepared to experiment with and modify the implementation of their professional knowledge and skills in order to continue their own learning. The learning which results is enhanced when the practitioner takes time to evaluate the outcomes. This can be done verbally, but it is often done in writing in order to maximize the reflection, and as part of building a record of the learning.

Reflective practice is particularly valuable for the beginning or transition phases of a career, when the professional is encountering many new experiences and wants to use them to enhance his or her knowledge. Reflective practice is therefore an ideal accompaniment to mentoring.

What Is a Learning Journal?

In order to gain maximum benefit from this style of learning, it is important that you take the time to reflect on both the process and outcomes of mentoring activities. Mentorees have a responsibility to help shape the mentoring experience to meet your needs. This can be achieved by reviewing each contact with your mentor and reflecting on the purpose of the meeting, the outcomes in terms of personal tasks or goals, and the learning which results.

For mentorees, a learning journal serves as
- a record of your mentoring relationship
- a means of reviewing your progress towards achieving your objectives
- a tool for reflecting on your mentoring activities
- a method for enhancing your learning.

For mentors, the learning journal can act as
- a record of your mentoring relationship
- a tool for developing your training and coaching skills
- a guide to your mentoree's progress
- a prompt for mentoring activities
- a portfolio of your teaching and learning work.

Learning without thought is labour lost; thought without learning is perilous
—Confucius

My favourite thing is to go where I've never been
—Diane Arbus

All growth is a leap in the dark, a spontaneous,
unpremeditated act without benefit of experience
—Henry Miller

It is good to have an end to journey towards; but it is the journey that matters in the end
—Ursula K. Le Guin

Spoon feeding in the long run teaches us nothing except the shape of the spoon
—E. M. Forster

The best careers advice to give the young is, find out what you like doing best and get someone to pay you for doing it
—Katherine Whilehaen

Thoroughly to teach another is the best way to teach yourself
—Tryon Edwards

*Life was meant to be lived and curiosity must be kept alive.
One must never, for whatever reason, turn one's back on life*
—Eleanor Roosevelt

There is no one right way to learn, since a match is needed between diverse opportunities and preferred learning styles
—Peter Honey

To achieve, you need thought . . . You have to know what you are doing and that's real power
—Ayn Rand

It may be a mistake to mix different wines, but old and new wisdom mix admirably
—Bertolt Brecht

*It is the soul's duty to be loyal to its own desires.
It must abandon itself to its master passion*
—Rebecca West

It is good to rub and polish our brain against that of others
—Montaigne

I can always be distracted by love, but eventually I get horny for my creativity
—Gilda Radner

*I'm not a teacher, only a fellow traveller whom you asked the way.
I pointed ahead–ahead of myself as well as of you*
    —George Bernard Shaw

*To appreciate openness, we must have experienced encouragement
to try the new, to seek alternatives, to view fresh possibilities*
—Sister Mary Luke Tobin

Learning is a treasure which accompanies the owner everywhere
—Chinese proverb

Coming together is a beginning; keeping together is progress; working together is success
—Henry Ford

The events in our lives happen in a sequence in time, but in their significance to ourselves, they find their own order . . . the continuous thread of revelation
—Eudora Welty

To teach is to learn twice
—Joseph Joubert

Those whom we support hold us up for life
—Marie Ebner von Eschenbach

Learning is but an adjunct to ourself. And where we are, our learning likewise is
—William Shakespeare

Patterns of the past echo in the present and resound through the future
—Dhyani Ywahoo

One must be thrust out of a finished cycle in life, and that leap [is] the most difficult to make–to part with one's faith, one's love, when one would prefer to renew the faith and recreate the passion
—Anaïs Nin

SECTION 3

MORE ABOUT MENTORING

Frequently Asked Questions (FAQs)

How do we start?
This will depend on the structure of the mentoring program, which may begin with an orientation session. It is then the responsibility of the mentor to initiate contact and set up the first meeting. After getting to know each other a little and if you decide that you want to continue, make sure that you agree to keep in touch regularly. (See *Section 1: The Seven Stages of Mentoring* for a general outline)

What do we do?
In short, it doesn't matter, so long as you do something—one of the critical factors in mentoring is that some type of activity takes place regularly. It may take a few meetings to clarify what arrangements will work best. Doing a project or working on a committee together is one of the best methods of practical mentoring.

How often should we be in contact?
This varies with the type of program—group mentoring meetings may be held at regular intervals, and individual partnerships or small group meetings may depend more on the needs of the mentoree and the extent of the mentor's input and available time. Practical considerations about how much time you have will influence where, when, and for how long you meet and whether you have contact in person, by phone, or by email. It may be a good idea to set up frequent short meetings or conversations to get off to a good start; later contact may be more ad hoc. Mentors, especially, need to remember the importance of follow-up meetings.

Is the relationship based on the mentoree's asking for help?
Yes, but not totally. Mentors need to take their commitment seriously and initiate meetings in the absence of particular problems. The mentoring relationship is not simply for emergency support (although it can be this as well).

What if the relationship seems nonproductive?
For a variety of personal and professional reasons, a mentoring relationship may not be productive. The relationship depends on trust and honesty, so all parties need to acknowledge it if the relationship is not what they expected. If any party feels this to be the case they should contact their organization's mentoring committee in order that other arrangements can be made.

How long does the relationship last?
This depends on the way in which the program is structured—it may be 12 months with the option of continuing. Mentoring is generally a long-term relationship, so it can last as long as it suits all parties.

How do I learn more about the roles and responsibilities of individuals in mentoring?
Training in mentoring and professional coaching is widely available. The notes and reading list at the end of this diary include relevant articles and books. Your research will reveal many other items, especially on the Internet. Members of your organization's mentoring committee are a resource for support, ideas, and feedback.

What are the benefits of mentoring?
The research literature is developing, and program evaluations are documenting the outcomes and showing benefits to mentorees, mentors, and their organizations. The most common benefit to mentorees is a feeling of being supported, but more objective assessments include improved career and psychosocial outcomes. The latest research shows that mentors benefit by being part of a group of mentors on whom they can draw for peer mentoring. For professional associations, mentoring has been shown to be useful in membership recruitment and retention.

What makes a good mentor?
Mentors must have good interpersonal skills and an interest in the development of others. Ideally they will have done some training in mentoring skills (professional coaching, giving and receiving feedback, goal setting, counseling), as these differ from normal communication skills. Mentors must be accessible and able to commit to regular contact and/or meetings.

What makes a good mentoree?
Mentorees share responsibility for making the relationship work—such as asking questions and trying different approaches. Negotiation and listening skills are also important.

What support can we expect from the organization or the mentoring program committee?
A facilitated mentoring program provides a clearly defined purpose and structure. There will also be resources in the form of committee support to facilitate effective mentoring relationships, a structure for initiating, maintaining, and concluding mentoring relationships, information and training in mentoring skills, some regular meetings for participants, and evaluation of the program's outcomes.

Mentoring and Change

The desire for a mentor often appears during times of transition. Studies of organizational behavior and change suggest that mentoring can help to ease the transition and alleviate stress.

Specific mentoring activities are appropriate to the phases associated with change.[6]

These phases are:
1. Optimism
2. Pessimism
3. Resistance
4. Acceptance and Commitment.

Phase 1: Optimism

People may have an unrealistic view of what is needed to accomplish the desired change and vision for the future.

Mentors can help mentorees understand what is needed by:
- asking questions that help people identify their reactions to change
- asking questions which identify the positive and negative aspects of the change
- providing some perspective by sharing their experiences of change, to make the experience real and possible.

Phase 2: Pessimism

People start questioning the need for change; discomfort and difficulties may be experienced.

Mentors can help mentorees explore possibilities and understand their feelings and behavior by:
- creating opportunities for sharing feelings and reflections
- giving open and honest feedback
- showing genuine caring and respect.

Phase 3: Resistance
People are unwilling to embrace the change.

The major roles of mentors are:
- to listen
- to help mentorees acknowledge and face obstacles
- to help mentorees recognize their reasons for resistance by giving feedback which supports and challenges, while always showing respect for the mentoree's position.

Phase 4: Acceptance and Commitment
People start to believe in the process and feel a part of it.

Mentors can:
- help mentorees formulate and commit to action plans
- help mentorees reflect on the stages of the change process and their learning
- celebrate successes
- recognize individual and group contributions.

Further Reading

Lacey, K., *Making mentoring happen*, Warriewood, NSW, Australia, Business and Professional Publishing, 1999.

McKenzie, B., *Friends in high places*, Sydney, Business and Professional Publishing, 1995.

MacLennan, N., *Coaching and mentoring*, Aldershot, Hampshire, England, Gower, 1995.

Murray, M., *Beyond the myths and magic of mentoring*, San Francisco, Jossey-Bass, 1991.

Parsloe, E. and C. Allen, *Learning for earning*, London, Institute of Personnel and Development, 1999.

Parsloe, Eric, *The manager as coach and mentor*, 2nd ed., London, Institute of Personnel and Development, 1999.

Rico, G.L., *Writing the natural way: using right-brain techniques to release your expressive powers*, New York, Jeremy P. Tarcher/Putnam Book, 1983.

Rolfe-Flett, A., *Develop your mentoring skills*, Kincumber South, NSW, Australia, Synergetic Management, 1998.

Rolfe-Flett, A., *The mentoring workbook*, Kincumber South, NSW, Australia, Synergetic Management, 1995.

Schön, Donald A., *Educating the reflective practitioner*, San Francisco, Jossey-Bass, 1987.

Scutt, J., *Living generously: women mentoring women*, Melbourne, Artemis, 1996.

Tye, M., *I need mentors—don't I?: a guide to finding and using multiple mentors*, Bunbury, WA, Australia, Australian Federation of Business and Professional Women, 1996.

Organizations

International Mentoring Association
This is a nonprofit organization which promotes the concept of mentoring. The association publishes a newsletter, *The mentoring connection*, and a members' directory and holds an annual conference in the United States.
Membership enquiries: cedu_ima@wmich.edu
http://www.mentoring-association.org
http://www.wmich.edu/conferences/mentoring/

Oxford School of Coaching and Mentoring
Contact: Eric Parsloe
Email: oscm@wolseyhall.co.uk

The Directory of Mentor Arts and Mentorship
http://www.peer.ca/mentor.html

NOTES

[1] Kram, K. E., & L. Isabella. "Mentoring alternatives: the role of peer relationships in career development," *The academy of management journal*, 28 (1985): 110-32.

[2] Adapted from MacLennan, N. *Coaching and mentoring*. Aldershot: Gower, 1995.

[3] Adapted from McKenzie, B. *Friends in high places*. Sydney: Business and Professional Publishing, 1995.

[4] This checklist is provided by Leonie Blair, AIMA Training and Consultancy Services, Canberra, ACT, Australia.

[5] Schön, Donald A. *Educating the reflective practitioner*. San Francisco: Jossey-Bass, 1987.

[6] Pyle, T. "Mentoring and change: creating an environment for successful transitions," *The mentoring connection* Winter 1999: 1, 5. http://www.wmich.edu/conferences/mentoring/

ABOUT THE AUTHORS

In 1995, Ann Ritchie and Paul Genoni established the Group Mentoring Program for graduate librarians as an initiative of the Western Australian branch of the Australian Library and Information Association.

In addition to practical experience in individual and group mentoring, the authors have researched and evaluated mentoring programs, published and presented internationally on the topic, and have developed a workshop ("How to Set Up a Facilitated Group Mentoring Program"). They have received awards for mentoring services to the library profession and to university graduates.

Ann Ritchie, B.App.Sci. (Information and Library Studies), Grad.Dip. (Health Promotion), M.Sc., is a library consultant and trainer.

Paul Genoni, B.A., Grad.Dip. (Information and Library Studies), M.A., Ph.D., is a lecturer at Curtin University of Technology, Australia.